The Little
Bug Spotters
Guide

Jaclyn Crupi

Alicat

Contents

How to spot bugs 4

Be besties with a bug **6**

Meet the bugs 8
Introducing insects 10
What do insects do? 11
Spiders 12
Moths and butterflies 14
Locusts, grasshoppers and crickets ... 16
Dragonflies and damselflies 17
Mantises 18
Flies and mosquitoes 19
Bees and wasps 20
Ants 22
Beetles 23
Bugs 24
Snails, centipedes and millipedes ... 25

How to spot bugs **26**

A bug hunt 28
How to catch a bug 30
Where bugs live 32
Bugs in a garden 34

Bugs in a desert   36
Bugs in a forest   38
Bugs in a pond   40
Bug bingo!   42

Bugs as pets   **44**
Which bug?   46
Basic bug care   48
Home for a bug   50
Food for a bug   52

Bug activities   **54**
Build a bug house   56
Bury a beetle bucket   57
Plant a hedge   58
Build a small pond   59
Attract butterflies   60
A bee hotel   61
Bug-friendly gardening   62
Build an ant farm   63
Happy bug spotting!   64

How to spot bugs

Being a little bug spotter is all about knowing when and where to look for all kinds of interesting bugs. It's also about knowing which bug is which! The best way to start your own bug spotting fun is to get outside. Bugs live everywhere; in your garden, in your local park, in the forest, in a pond, in the desert and sometimes in your own home!

You'll need some simple equipment before you can get started bug spotting.

Little bug spotters clothes

Sunscreen – to protect your skin from burning in the hot sun

Gumboots – to keep your feet dry while exploring outside

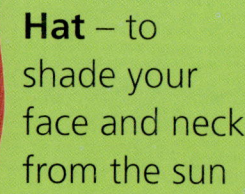

Hat – to shade your face and neck from the sun

Little bug spotters tools

Magnifying glass – to help you spot and see small bugs

Clean jars with air holes – to keep your bugs

Butterfly net – to catch flying bugs

Soil sifter – to help find crawly bugs

Bug catcher – to catch all kinds of bugs

Torch – to help you see during after dark bug spotting

Digital camera (if your family has one) – to record the bugs you spot

Safety first

When busy bug spotting, be sure to always stay close to an adult and always let someone know where you're going.

Some bugs bite or sting so always check with an adult before touching or picking up bugs.

Whenever you see the 'I bite' or the 'I sting' warning in this book, take extra care with these bugs.

Be besties with a bug

Once you've read this chapter, jump into your gumboots, grab your magnifying glass and explore the amazing bug world that's just outside!

There are lots of bugs out there for you to spot. But before you can spot them you need to know a little bit about them such as where they live, what they eat and what they spend their time doing.

The information on the following pages will show different kinds of bugs and what the differences are between them. You'll also find out where they live so you can better spot them!

Meet the bugs 8

Introducing insects 10

What do insects do? 11

Spiders 12

Moths and butterflies 14

Locusts, grasshoppers and crickets 16

Dragonflies and damselflies 17

Mantises 18

Flies and mosquitoes 19

Bees and wasps 20

Ants 22

Beetles 23

Bugs 24

Snails, centipedes and millipedes 25

Meet the bugs

Insects, centipedes, spiders and other creepy-crawlies are often called bugs. Bugs live all over the world. They have three things in common:

❋ Their bodies are broken into sections, sometimes by what looks like rings

❋ They have jointed legs and antennae poking from their heads

❋ They have a hard outer covering

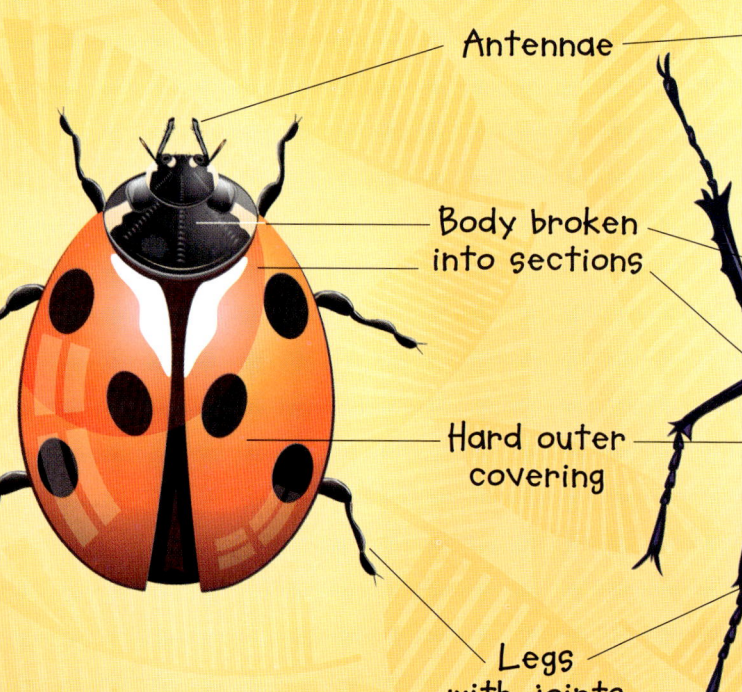

Antennae

Body broken into sections

Hard outer covering

Legs with joints

Brilliant bug fact!

Some bugs live near water but no bugs spend all their time in the water.

What makes a bug a bug!

There are four main groups of bugs (and we'll look at all of them in this book):

❈ Insects (ants, beetles, butterflies, bees, etc.)

❈ Arachnids (spiders, scorpions, mites, etc.)

❈ Millipedes (plant-eaters with two sets of legs on each body section)

❈ Centipedes (meat-eaters with one set of legs on each body section)

What this all means is that there are lots of interesting bugs for us to find out about. In fact, there are millions of different bugs in the world and more being discovered all the time! So let's start to take a closer look at some of these amazing bugs.

Introducing insects

Insects are one of the groups of bugs, but not all bugs are insects. Insects live everywhere in the world except for very high up in the icy North and South Poles and near volcanoes.

Most insects have one or two pairs of wings although some insects, such as lice and fleas, have no wings at all.

Insect body parts

head

thorax

abdomen

Brilliant bug fact!

All insects are cold-blooded.

How an ant grows up

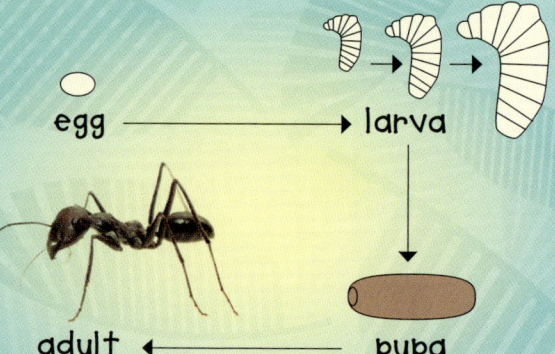

egg ⟶ larva

↓

adult ⟵ pupa

Brilliant bug fact!

There are about one million types of insects living in the world today.

What do insects do?

Insects are special for all living things on Earth. They might be small but they have big and important jobs.

Insects and plants and flowers

Insects spread pollen, which is a fine powder in plants that the plants need to reproduce. Pollen can float to a female flower in the wind but it is mostly carried there by insects. All living things rely on plants so this is a very important job for insects. Bees play a big role in spreading pollen to fruit trees and flower blossoms.

Insects and soil

Insects help us by adding air to the soil which keeps soil healthy. Digging bugs, such as ants and beetles, dig tunnels that make paths for water through the soil.

Spiders

Most people don't realise how amazing and interesting spiders are and instead are afraid of them. Some spiders bite so it is best to be careful of them but mostly spiders are just really interesting. Let's take a closer look.

I bite!

Brown Spider

What are spiders?

eight legs

Trapdoor Spider

I bite!

Spiders belong to a group of animals called arachnids, say *ah-rac-nids* (they are not insects). They have two body sections, eight legs, no wings or antennae and are not able to chew.

two body sections

Are they dangerous?

All spiders have fangs! And, yes, almost all of them have venom or spider poison in them. Lucky for us, most spider poison will not harm people because it is quite weak and many spiders can't bite people. Most spiders use their venom to stop an insect from moving. For other spiders, their poison is strong enough to kill their prey. There are a few spiders with poison strong enough to hurt us.

Dangerous spiders

Watch out for these and stay well away. They have strong venom and they bite easily. Never try to touch spiders and if you see one call an adult.

We bite!

Black Widow

Funnel Web

Tiny spiders

Spotting tiny spiders can be hard. Most spiders are small but some spiders are VERY small.

Hairy spiders

Lots of people think hairy spiders are the most dangerous because of how they look. They do bite but really, they're just hairy.

I bite!

Tarantula

Spider spotting tips

✽ Look in dark corners, under furniture and in cracks and crevices.

✽ Many spiders will only come out at night so try to do some of your searching when it is getting dark! Use a torch.

13

Moths and butterflies

Moths are much more common than butterflies but most people love butterflies because of their brightly coloured wings.

Moth

What are moths and butterflies?

Moths and butterflies are flying insects. They have many things in common and some differences. The main difference between moths and butterflies is that butterflies come out during the day and moths are usually found after dark.

Butterfly

Caterpillars

Before changing into beautiful butterflies and moths they start as eggs and then become caterpillars. You can spot caterpillars on plant leaves. Caterpillars can be many different sizes and colours. Some have spots, some have spikes and some look hairy!

Butterfly and moth spotting tips

※ Butterflies are easiest to spot in the warmer months.

※ Know their favourite places. Butterflies can be found in fields, mountains and parks. They can also be seen in gardens, near ponds or right outside your door.

※ Butterflies love nectar and can often be spotted near flowers.

※ Spray your hand with sugar water. Butterflies have a sweet tooth and will often land right on your hand to take a sip.

※ To best spot moths, turn a light on outside once it's dark. They will fly straight towards it.

Hairy caterpillars

Locusts, grasshoppers and crickets

Locusts, grasshoppers and crickets are similar insects that all make sounds by rubbing their wings together or against their legs.

Help for spotting locusts, grasshoppers and crickets

* You might need to look carefully as they are hard to see when sitting on a plant.
* Follow the sounds they make – a sure thing to lead you right to them!
* Swarms of locusts are so big that they would be very hard not to notice!
* Grasshoppers are easiest to spot in summer.
* Crickets like to spend time under stones, so turn some over and see what you find.

What are locusts?

Locusts can change colour and travel very fast in big groups. They can also breed very quickly. Swarms of locusts can destroy huge crops.

What are grasshoppers?

Grasshoppers are hopping insects that are active during the day. Their antennae are almost always shorter than their bodies.

What are crickets?

Crickets have flattened bodies and long antennae. They come out at night.

Dragonflies and damselflies

Dragonflies are some of the fastest insects in the world. It's hard to tell but the top speed of a dragonfly is about 90 kilometres per hour.

What are dragonflies?

Dragonflies are insects with two sets of wings which they flap super fast (about 30 times per second). A dragonfly can see all the way around itself. A female dragonfly lays her eggs on a plant in the water, or she will just drop them into the water.

What are damselflies?

Damselflies are very similar to dragonflies only smaller. They hold their wings differently when resting and they are weaker fliers than dragonflies. Their eyes are separated whereas dragonfly eyes are joined.

Spot those dragonflies and damselflies

* Dragonflies and damselflies spend time near water so look near ponds and lakes.

* Dragonflies and damselflies fly a lot so they are bound to be found in the open air in parks and gardens.

* Dragonflies and damselflies love the sun and spend lots of time in sunny places.

I bite!

Mantises

Mantises are sometimes referred to as 'praying mantises' because they often stand in a way that looks like they are praying.

What are mantises?

Mantises can hide themselves by changing colour. The colour can be from dark brown to green which helps them blend into tree bark or green plant leaves. Mantises eat other insects and sometimes even small reptiles or birds!

Meet a mantis

* Mantises are good at hiding so use your magnifying glass to help spot them on bark or plants.

* Only try to spot them in the warmest months.

* They like to eat insects so you might see them in areas where there are lots of other insects.

All about me

Name: Mantis

Average size: 5–10 cm

Where to spot them: In very warm areas among grasses and bark

What they eat: Mostly insects

Flies and mosquitoes

Flies and mosquitoes are very common and super easy to spot.

What is a fly?

Flies have two wings (most insects have four wings). Like all insects they have six legs and their body has three parts. There are more than 100,000 types of flies. Flies live all over the world.

What is a mosquito?

Like flies, mosquitoes have two wings but have scales on their wings. Female mosquitoes' mouths form a long sucker which can pierce the skin of plants and animals. Males are different from females and have feathery antennae and are not able to bite.

All about me

Name: Fly

Where to spot them: Everywhere and anywhere

What they eat: Plant nectar and other liquids

Babies: Females lay 75 to 100 eggs

All about me

Name: Mosquito

Where to spot them: Everywhere

What they eat: Plant nectar and blood (females only)

Babies: Females lay eggs on the surface of water

I bite!

What is nectar?

Nectar is a sweet liquid made by flowers and eaten by some insects and birds.

Bees and wasps

Bees and wasps are common and easy to see in many gardens and parks. There are many different kinds of bees and wasps.

What is a bee?

A bee is an insect that carries pollen from plants and makes honey. Some bees are worker bees, some are queen bees and some are drones. They each do different jobs.

Bees usually build their nests in trees but will sometimes build them in attics or chimneys.

Honeybee

sting!

All about me

Name: Honeybee

Average size: 1 cm

Where to spot them: In gardens and parks near flowers

What they eat: Nectar and pollen

Babies: A queen honeybee can lay more than 1,000 eggs per day

The buzz about bees and wasps

❋ Bees and wasps love flowers so start looking for them where there are a lot of flowers.

❋ Look in sunny spots as both bees and wasps like to be in the sun.

❋ Look for nests in trees (but be careful, stay away and never ever touch or move a nest).

What is a wasp?

Wasps are stinging insects that carry pollen and eat and kill lots of other insects. Keep clear of them and their nests as they can get mad and sting you.

Wasps build their nests in trees and other places where they are not likely to be disturbed.

All about me

Name: Yellowjacket/hornet

Average size: 3 cm

Where to spot them: In gardens and parks

What they eat: Spiders, leaves and insects

Babies: Females lay about 50 eggs

I sting!

Yellowjacket wasp

Ants

They might be very small, but ants are really strong insects; they can lift things 20 times heavier than they are! They are also very busy insects, always rushing from place to place.

Leaf cutter ant

What is an ant?

An ant is a small, crawling insect that lives in a big group. There are many different kinds of ants. Some bite, some have wings and some build nests in wood.

All about me

Name: Pavement ant
Length: 0.4 cm

bite!

Where to spot them: On pavements and around your house
What they eat: Almost anything, including insects, grease, seeds, honeydew, honey, bread, meats, nuts and cheese

All about me

Name: Carpenter ant

bite!

Length: 2 cm
Where to spot them: Near dead, damp wood
What they eat: Only liquids like honeydew and sap

Beetles

There are so many different kinds of beetles that there is no way we could talk about them all. They come in lots of shapes and sizes!

What is a beetle?

All beetles have a hard shell and wings. Most beetles have shells that cover their whole body but some have very small shells. It might be hard to see some beetles' wings, but they're there.

The good guys

Ladybirds are the 'good guys' in the garden as they gobble up aphids and scale insects that eat and ruin plants and flowers.

All about me

Name: Ladybird/ ladybug or lady beetle
Length: 0.8 cm
Where to spot them: On leaves and flying around
What they eat: Insects and plants

All about me

Name: Weevil
Length: Less than 0.6 cm
Where to spot them: On farms
What they eat: Grain, cotton and plants

All about me

Name: Dung beetle/scarab beetle
Average size: 3 cm
Where to spot them: Anywhere there is animal droppings
What they eat: Animal droppings

Bugs

These bugs all have mouths they can suck from. So while they're cool to look at, it's not fun if they bite you.

This is one bug that we hope you never spot as they're a real pest.

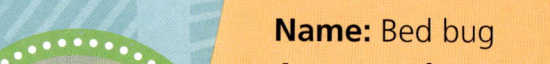

All about me

Name: Bed bug
Average size: 0.6 cm
Where to spot them: Under mattresses and in couches
What they eat: Blood

All about me

Name: Stink bug
Average size: 2 cm
Where to spot them: Orchards, gardens and farms
What they eat: Leaves, caterpillars, flowers, fruit and crops

All about me

Name: Cicada/jar fly/July fly
Average size: 3 cm
Where to spot them: At nighttime near light or wherever you hear their sound
What they eat: Liquids

What's all that noise?

Cicadas are the noisiest insect in the world. They make noise to protect themselves from birds who like to eat them.

Snails, centipedes and millipedes

These three animals are usually easy to find in the garden.

What are snails?

Snails have a hard shell and a soft body. They like to live in gardens so they can eat plants. That's why gardeners don't like them very much. The best way to spot a snail is to put your gumboots on and go into the garden just after it has rained.

What are centipedes and millipedes?

Centipedes and millipedes are bugs with lots of legs! They like to live in gardens and compost piles. They sometimes come inside homes but they do no harm as they only eat insects.

Millipede

Centipede

25

How to spot bugs

Once you've read this chapter, you're ready to use your little bug spotter skills!

Now you know what some bugs look like, it's time to find out all you need to know to spot them.

There are a lot of bugs out there, so just follow these tips and with a little bit of patience you'll soon be showing your family and friends all the great bugs you have spotted.

A bug hunt 28

How to catch a bug 30

Where bugs live 32

Bugs in a garden 34

Bugs in a desert 36

Bugs in a forest 38

Bugs in a pond 40

Bug bingo! 42

A bug hunt

So let's go on a bug hunt! We won't have to go very far. We'll search for creepy-crawlies, buzzing bees, jumping spiders, tiny ants and giant dragonflies. We'll look high and low, under rocks and near water. We'll spot them, watch them, catch them and find out all about them.

How to bug hunt

❉ **Bug group**

It's fun to hunt bugs with friends. Make sure that between all of you, you have enough equipment.

- Containers to store bugs in
- Magnifying glass to get a closer look
- Net to catch them with
- Torch to see them in dark places

❉ **Be bug alert**

Make sure you tell the group about any dangerous bugs in your area and that they should be careful. The last thing you want is for someone to get bitten or stung by a bug.

✽ Get outside

The best places to look for bugs are in small cracks, under pots, logs, rocks and in piles of leaves. You'll have to be on your toes as bugs move fast! Give everyone something to hold so you all have a job to do. What a team!

✽ Bug magic

Remember that some bugs are excellent at blending in with their surroundings. You might need to spend extra time looking closely to see teeny tiny bugs. This is where your magnifying glass will really come in handy.

Look all around

Make sure you look up, down and all around. Bugs live everywhere. Look on tree branches, under leaves, on the outside of your house and in the air.

Bug journal

Write down the types of bugs you see in a notebook. Keep adding more as you spot them.

How to catch a bug

So you've been busy spotting lots of bugs and you decide you'd like to keep one for a while and take a closer look. You just need to catch it first! Some bugs are easier to catch than others. You'll need a few things ready to catch a bug:

- Clean, washed jars with air holes in the lids
- Butterfly net (if you have one)
- Bug catcher (if you have one)

Catching a spotted bug

❊ **Spotted!**

Once you have spotted a bug, don't loose sight of it, it might just disappear!

❊ **Flying**

If the bug is flying, catch it with your net. Gently scoop the insect out of the net with a jar and put the lid on tight.

❋ Crawling

To catch a crawling bug, put the open end of the jar over the bug. Slide a piece of paper between the bug and the ground. Tip the jar over, remove the paper and put the lid on. Easy!

Make your own bug jars

Wash some used jars, rinse well and take off any labels. Get an adult to poke air holes in the lids. Put some grass in the bottom of the jars. Now you're ready to go bug catching!

Setting a bug trap

To set a bug trap, dig a hole in the soil deep enough for a jar to be completely buried with the top of it level with the soil. Put some sugar in the jar to attract insects and leave it in the ground for a few days. You'll be amazed at how many bugs have crawled inside.

Where bugs live

Bugs live everywhere but we're going to look at the four most common places where you can find bugs:

- In a garden
- In a desert
- In a forest
- In a pond

Gardens

We all spend time in gardens and parks. Now that you know what to look for and where to look you will start to see lots of bugs every time you're in a garden or a park.

Deserts

Not many people live in the desert but you might visit sand dunes at a beach. Lots of bugs live there! They're hard to spot as they are usually the same colour as the sand but their tracks in the sand show where they have been.

Forests

Bugs just love plants and trees. Forests and rainforests also have lots of water which bugs like. You can spot lots of different kinds of bugs in these places.

Ponds

Some bugs need to live near water and might even lay their eggs in water. The most likely place to see these bugs is near ponds and lakes. Be on close bug watch next time you're near a pond.

Places to look

✳ In the air
✳ Around water
✳ In soil
✳ On or near pet animals
✳ In compost piles
✳ Around objects such as outdoor chairs or slides
✳ Near light globes at night
✳ Close to food
✳ Under rocks and stones
✳ On plants, flowers, trees, leaves and wood

Safety note

Always be extra careful near water and only go there with an adult.

Bugs in a garden

You'll find lots of insects and other bugs in a garden or park. There is lots for them to do here. They are busy finding food – plants and other insects or nectar from flowers. Gardens and parks are also safe places for them to lay their eggs.

Bug returning

You know how to catch these bugs now. They can't live for a long time in jars. Once you have finished watching them, making notes and taking photos, be sure to let the bugs out back into the garden where they belong.

Snail race

It's not unusual to find a large collection of snails under an old plank of wood. If you do, you can hold a snail race! Carefully take the snails from the wood and place them on the ground in a row. Time them for five minutes and whoever travels the furthest wins.

Bugs you might see easily

Caterpillars

Flies

Butterflies

Snails

Ants

Bugs harder to find

Spiders

Dragonflies

Centipedes

Beetles

Millipedes

Spot the bugs

Can you spot all ten bugs in this garden?

Bugs in a desert

Bugs can live in places that are dry, hot and cold – places like a desert. The desert might look empty but many little critters live there. Desert bugs are often the same colour as the sand or plants and can be very hard to spot. You need to look for bugs in a different way when you're in the desert.

Spotting desert bugs

A good tip is to look for bug trails in the sand. Usually a trail will lead you to where the bug is living. Many desert insects can drag food, which can be much bigger than they are, back to their home. Stand still and look carefully to see if you can see anything moving on the desert sand.

Bugs you might see easily

Locusts

Grasshoppers

Butterflies

Mosquitoes

Ants

Beetles

Bugs harder to find

Spiders

Mantises

Cicadas

Scorpions

Spot the bugs

Can you spot all ten
bugs in this desert?

Bugs in a forest

Insects are the largest group of animals in forests and rainforests. They like the warmth and the type of plants that live there. There is also lots of water.

Spotting forest bugs

Many bugs can be seen easily in forests and rainforests. Butterflies happily fly from place to place. Ants busily crawl along the forest floor and up the trunks of trees. Other bugs, such as mantises and dragonflies, are more difficult to spot. Mantises are the same colour as leaves and bark and dragonflies fly very quickly.

Growing, growing, growing!

Some insects can grow very large in rainforests, much larger than they do in other areas. This is because it is warm and there is plenty of food for them. This can make them easier to spot. Some beetles can be as big as your hand!

Bugs you might see easily

Caterpillars

Butterflies

Moths

Flies

Mosquitoes

Beetles

Ants

Bugs harder to find

Stick insects

Dragonflies

Damselflies

Spot the bugs

Can you spot all ten bugs in this rainforest?

Bugs in a pond

Only visit a pond with an adult. Even shallow water can be dangerous.

A pond is a small lake. The water is quite still and not very deep. This makes it a perfect place for insects to lay their eggs.

Spotting bugs near ponds

Many of the bugs that live in and near ponds are really small and you might need a magnifying glass to see some of them. They include beetles, dragonflies, snails and even water scorpions.

Water nets

The easiest way to see bugs in a pond is to scoop some up out of the water with your net. Look for tiny larvae (insect eggs). Empty them into a jar for a closer look. When you've finished with them, put them back into the pond where they belong.

Bugs you might see easily

Beetles

Flies

Snails

Ants

Butterflies

Caterpillars

Bugs harder to find

Stick insects

Dragonflies

Damselflies

Scorpions

Spot the bugs

Can you spot all ten
bugs near this pond?

Bug bingo!

On your bug hunts have you spotted these bugs? If you have, place a tick in the box. Count up all your ticks and be amazed by how many bugs you have spotted already!

❋ **A pale butterfly** ☑ Spotted

❋ **A colourful butterfly** ☐ Spotted

❋ **A caterpillar** ☐ Spotted

❋ **An ant** ☑ Spotted

❋ **A ladybird/ladybug** ☑ Spotted

❋ **A bee** ☑ Spotted

❋ **A dragonfly** ☐ Spotted

❄ **A mantis** ☐ Spotted

❄ **A spider** ☑ Spotted

❄ **A snail** ☐ Spotted

❄ **A centipede** ☐ Spotted

❄ **A millipede** ☐ Spotted

❄ **A fly** ☐ Spotted

❄ **A beetle** ☐ Spotted

❄ **A mosquito** ☐ Spotted

❄ **A cricket** ☐ Spotted

TOTAL: 4 ☑ **Spotted**

Bingo!

Bugs as pets

Bugs are great to spot but they are difficult to really get to know. Perhaps the answer is to keep a bug as a pet.

Now that you're a super little bug spotter, you might want to think about having a bug as a pet. Many bugs make great pets. Keeping a bug as a pet is also one of the best ways to learn about bugs. Bugs are usually quiet, clean pets who do not take up much space and are easy to look after.

You can buy many bugs as pets but it's more fun to catch them yourself!

Which bug?	46
Basic bug care	48
Home for a bug	50
Food for a bug	52

Which bug?

Choosing a bug for a pet is a big decision. There are lots of different things to think about before you decide which bug to get. Some grow really big, some make noise and some live for a long time.

Where will it live?

The first thing to think about is where the bug will live. A big glass or plastic container is enough for most bugs. Some prefer screened cages while others fly so you may need a lid on your bug container.

Get information!

If you want to keep a happy bug you must know all of this information

- Where does it like to live?
- What does it eat?
- Does it need water?
- Does it need a warm or cool room?
- How long does it live for?
- Does it like company?

Trial pet

It's probably smart to start with a small bug from your yard in a small container to see if you want to care for a bug.

Buy your bug

There are lots of stores that sell bugs for pets. Find a good one and ask them lots of questions about your bug before you take it home. Some bugs can be bought as babies (larvae) and raised.

Basic bug care

All pet bugs need three important things:

- ✽ Food and water
- ✽ A safe place to live
- ✽ Things that are similar to where they come from

All of these things depend on the bug. Most bugs don't like to be touched and handled. Some bugs, such as mantises, are very delicate and fragile and are easily hurt. Others can be dangerous. Make sure you know a lot about your bug.

What they're used to

If your bug is most active at night, then you should feed it at night. If the bug usually lives in warm areas then you should make sure it is always warm. If your bug eats plants then you should feed it plants. It's most important to make sure your bug feels at home.

No escape

It's important to make sure that your bug cannot escape from its new home. Many bugs can crawl and jump so your container needs to have a lid. All bugs need to breathe so don't forget air holes in the lid.

Pet bug safety

Never feed your pet bug with leaves or twigs that have been sprayed with insecticide and never spray the room that they are kept in with fly spray.

Always wash your hands after handling insects or soil.

Home for a bug

These are the sorts of homes that your bugs need.

Beetles

Beetles are the easiest bug to keep. They are happy in a glass fish tank or large jar with a mesh lid. Put 5 cm of potting mix in the base for them to burrow into.

Cockroaches and crickets

These bugs are very happy in a large glass tank or plastic container with a mesh lid to stop them escaping. They need a deep mixture of peat moss and clean sand on the base of the container and dried leaves on top for them to burrow into.

Caterpillars

A caterpillar home can be as easy as a tall glass jar with air holes in the lid. If the caterpillar turns into a butterfly, it's best to let it go as it will never be happy in a container.

Stick insects

These insects need a tall home as a jar of water must be placed at the bottom to hold small branches and leaves. Cover the jar with mesh as stick insects can't swim! Keep their home in a warm place.

Snails and millipedes

Snails get bored so they need an interesting home which is clean, fresh and damp. Use a plastic tank with a strong lid and plenty of air holes. Line the floor with compost or moss and decorate it with sticks, tree bark and plastic pots so they have somewhere to hide and for the millipedes to burrow.

Food for a bug

These are the foods that your bugs like to eat.

Beetles

Beetles love fresh food, particularly juicy fruit like banana. Change the fruit every day. Mist the air with a water spray each day.

Cockroaches and crickets

These insects love dried native leaves from the plants you found them on and a mist of water every day. A treat would be a little carrot and fresh fruit or oats. They can drink from a wet cotton wool ball if thirsty.

Caterpillars

Feed these with the same plant leaves you found them living on. Spray water into the jar or cage daily.

Snails and millipedes

The best food for snails is lettuce and cucumber but apple, banana and cabbage can also be given. They also need calcium. Millipedes feed happily on soil or peat-free compost mixed with dead leaves. This can be added to by giving all sorts of food items from the kitchen such as potato peelings.

Stick insects

Spray these insects 2 to 5 times a day with water. They eat fresh leaves from the plant you found them on.

Bug activities

Once you've read this chapter, you'll be ready and inspired to do lots of bug activities.

Now you know which bug is which and where to look for them, spotting bugs will be easier. There are a lot of fun things you can do to attract bugs to your garden. You can do these activities at home or talk to your teacher about doing them at school.

Get ready to be busy, little bug spotter!

Build a bug house   56

Bury a beetle bucket   57

Plant a hedge   58

Build a small pond   59

Attract butterflies   60

A bee hotel   61

Bug-friendly gardening   62

Build an ant farm   63

Happy bug spotting!   64

Build a bug house

You will need an adult to help you.

You will need:

- 4 equal-sized pieces of wood
- 1 piece of wood for the back of the box
- Wood saw
- Nails and hammer
- Drill and drill bit
- Wood screw

Make a bug house for insects and other bugs. This bug house is perfect for all flying bugs.

How to do it:

1. Make a simple box of timber. You will need four pieces of wood of equal length for the sides and one square piece for the back.
2. Drill a hole in the back of your box and screw it to a fence, wall or tree in a sheltered part of the garden.
3. From the front, fill your box with twigs, leaves, hollow branches and pieces of wood.

Even simpler

Take a bundle of bamboo canes or other twigs and tie them together with a piece of string. Hang up the bundle under the branch of a tree or to a railing and the bugs will start to move in.

Bury a beetle bucket

This is an easy way to make a home for all sorts of beetles.

You will need an adult to help you.

How to do it:

1. Make large holes all around the bucket. Leave 5 cm between each hole.
2. Make 5 similar holes in the bottom of the bucket.
3. Put several large stones in the bottom of the bucket then fill it with a mixture of woodchips and soil. Use 4 times more woodchips than soil.
4. Dig a hole in the garden where you think beetles might live and bury the bucket right up to its top. Fill in the gaps around the side with soil.
5. Leave it alone for a few months (except for adding more woodchips if needed).
6. Carefully sift through the bucket to see the beetles you have made a home for.

You will need:

- Soft, plastic bucket
- Tool for punching large (3 cm) holes – this should only be done by an adult
- Bag of woodchips
- Large stones
- Soil

Even simpler

Buy a beetle bucket with holes already in it.

Plant a hedge

You will need an adult to help you.

You will need:

- Hedge plants
- Shovel
- Compost or other fertiliser

Hundreds of bugs live in and feed from hedges. Hedges make a safe place for bugs to live. Talk to your parents about the idea of planting a hedge in the garden.

How to do it:

1. Choose the area in the garden where the hedge will go.
2. Dig holes close together for all the plants you have. Read the plant labels to know how deep the holes should be.
3. Plant them in double rows if you have the space.
4. Fertilise and water the plants. Now you just have to wait for them to grow.
5. Clip the hedge to shape as it grows.
6. The best way to see some of the bugs that call your hedge home is to gently tap the hedge with a stick and hold a sheet of paper underneath to catch the bugs.

Build a small pond

You will need an adult to help you.

Make a small pond or water feature! Still water attracts dragonflies and damselflies as well as other water-loving insects.

How to do it:

1. Place your container in a sunny part of the garden.
2. Fill the container with water. Rainwater is by far the best water for your pond. If you use tap water, let it stand for a few days first.
3. Choose native water plants (talk to someone at your local plant nursery). Put them in the container.
4. Sit back and wait for the dragonflies and damselflies to arrive!

You will need:

- A large container
- Water
- Water plants

59

Attract butterflies

You will need an adult to help you.

You will need:

- Coloured card
- Scissors
- Glue
- Plastic bottle top
- Cotton wool
- A stick
- Sugar
- A pen
- A plant pot

Try this!

You can also make a butterfly feeder.

The easiest way to see butterflies in your garden is to plant the shrubs and flowers they prefer. Butterflies love nectar from these plants and will come a long way for a sugary drink!

Flowers do not come out all year, so when your garden is bare, you can attract butterflies with these nifty paper flowers.

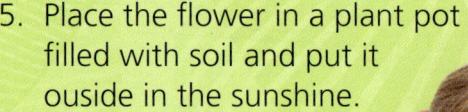

How to do it:

1. Draw a flower on the card and cut it out. Ask an adult for help.
2. Stick the bottle top on the front of the flower and the stick on the back.
3. Mix some sugar in hot water then soak some cotton wool in the sugary water.
4. Glue the cotton wool inside the bottle top.
5. Place the flower in a plant pot filled with soil and put it ouside in the sunshine.

A bee hotel

You will need an adult to help you.

Female bees are always searching for somewhere to lay their eggs, so why don't you make a bee hotel for them.

How to do it:

1. Get an adult to help you cut the bamboo and hollow wood into lengths that are the same length as the box. The wood needs to be straight so that the female bee can lay a number of eggs in each hollow.

2. Carefully pack the frame of the bee hotel with the stems until it is tightly packed. The front of your box will now look like honeycomb.

3. Hang your bee hotel on a sunny wall, sheltered from the rain, and wait for the bees to investigate it in the spring.

You will need:

- Small, old, wooden crate
- Enough bamboo, twigs, straight hollow plant stems and tree branches to fill the crate

Bees can sting when they get angry so never, ever disturb their hotel!

Bug-friendly gardening

There are lots of things you can do to make sure your garden is super bug friendly.

Wild corner

Letting a part of your garden go a bit wild is a sure way to attract bugs. Bugs love hollow tree trunks, stones and stick piles lying around. Insects of all types are sure to use your wild area to live in, feed, lay eggs in and spread pollen.

Gardening for bugs

Try to only use natural and organic fertilisers and soils in the garden. These are better for the environment and much healthier for bugs.

Flowers all year round

Many bugs love flowers so plant different types of plants to make sure you have flowers all year round. This will keep your bugs happy and your garden will look beautiful.

Build an ant farm

Ants can be great fun to watch and they are really easy to keep. Only keep them for two to three days at a time, ants really belong in the garden.

How to do it:

1. Cover the outside of a jar with coloured paper and hold in place with masking tape. Fill with soil from your garden.
2. Dig up an ant nest in your yard and try to find the biggest ant (that will be the queen). Wear gloves because the worker ants will try to defend her.
3. Put the queen in the glass jar with as many worker ants as you can collect.
4. Stretch some fine gauze material over the top and hold in place with a rubber band.
5. Feed the ants every day with a little honey sprinkled on the soil surface.
6. Keep peeping behind the paper to see how they are going – ants are really busy insects and soon you will see their tunnels against the glass.

You will need:

- Clean, empty, large jar
- Square of fine gauze material large enough to cover top of jar
- Rubber band
- Soil
- Dark coloured paper
- Masking tape
- Gardening gloves
- Honey

Happy bug spotting!

Now you know everything about bugs and are a proper little bug spotter! So get out there and enjoy spotting the bugs you know so much about. You are a true bug expert and can show your family and friends everything you now know about bugs.